DUNGEONS & TOMBS

DUNGEONS & DRAGONS

DUNGEONS & TOMBS

A Young Adventurer's Guide

WRITTEN BY JIM ZUB

WITH STACY KING AND ANDREW WHEELER

TEN SPEED PRESS
California | New York

CONTENTS

BUILDING YOUR OWN DUNGEON

INTRODUCTION

Dungeons and tombs are places filled with adventure. Every door, a new mystery to be unearthed. Every encounter, a chance for victory or disaster.

This book is a tour through some of the most frightening and fatal places in the world of DUNGEONS & DRAGONS. It's a guide to their masters and myths, their creatures and corridors. It will show you six lethal lairs, introduce you to the beasts that live within, and then teach you how to construct your own diabolical dungeon.

Read this book from start to finish, or open it to any spot, get entranced by the cool artwork, and start your journey there. The more you read, the more you'll discover. The more you discover, the easier it will be to imagine your own heroic tales as you and your friends explore the unknown and gather hidden treasures.

Will your quest lead to fame, fortune, and songs sung of your deeds, or will your legend be lost in the shadow-filled crypts that have claimed countless other heroes? In the end, that's up to you. DUNGEONS & DRAGONS is all about unique adventures, and yours is about to begin.

Be brave!

PREPARING FOR YOUR DUNGEON DELVE

Before you head into the darkness, ready to explore and fight creatures fearsome and foul, you'll want to do a bit of preparation. Dungeon delving is a dangerous occupation. Adventurers with a bit of foresight and a plan tend to survive longer than those who charge empty-headedly into the unknown. Courage is good. Courage and the right tools for the job are even better. Think about these questions and then get ready for your journey.

- Who is in your adventuring party? Are you traveling alone or in a group? Check "Your Adventuring Party" on the facing page for some options, or build a more detailed set of characters using the *Warriors & Weapons* or *Wizards & Spells* books, which may also inform answers to the other questions.

- Where are you going? A cave, a castle, a swamp, a scorching desert, an undersea lair, a boneyard, or somewhere else? If the trek looks like it will be a long one, you'll want to make sure you bring bedrolls, blankets, a tent, and a way to light a fire. Are you prepared to hunt for food and forage for your meals, or are you bringing rations?

- What climate might you encounter once you get there? Hot or cold, bright or dark, wet or dry? Each possibility requires different clothing to stay comfortable. Can you see in the dark? If not, do you have a light source you can count on?

- Do you have a map of, or other knowledge about, the dungeon you seek? Any information at all is better than heading into a complete mystery. Legends, rumors, or local gossip may all prove helpful as you delve into fortresses, ruins, caverns, or crypts.

YOUR ADVENTURING PARTY

In DUNGEONS & DRAGONS, you and your friends take on the roles of adventurers who have banded together to fight monsters and gather treasure. Each hero will have their own special skills, determined by their character class. Here are a few of the most common types of heroes and their unique abilities.

- **Barbarian** Fierce, primal warriors capable of entering a mighty battle rage.

- **Bard** Magical entertainers who can inspire, heal, and create illusions through their performances.

- **Cleric** Faithful warriors who wield divine magic in service of a higher power.

- **Druid** Shapeshifting guardians who draw upon the power of nature.

- **Fighter** Soldiers and mercenaries trained in a variety of weapons and armor.

- **Monk** Masters of the martial arts who use mystic energy to empower their attacks.

- **Paladin** Holy champions who combine divine magic with martial skill.

- **Ranger** Scouts and trappers who blend fighting skills with keen knowledge of their surroundings to protect the wilderness.

- **Rogue** Thieves, acrobats, and explorers who specialize in stealth and trickery to overcome obstacles.

- **Sorcerer** Spellcasters whose power comes from their magical birthright.

- **Warlock** Magicians who gain their power through pacts with otherworldly creatures.

- **Wizard** Scholarly magic users who can manipulate reality itself.

THE MOST DANGEROUS DUNGEONS

A head lie six strange and sinister spaces ready to be uncovered by you and your fellow adventurers. Each dungeon profile covers the following important information:

OVERVIEW Background lore on the location, its purpose, and who currently controls it.

IMPORTANT PLACES Key regions within the dungeon that may help or hinder you on your journey.

SPOTLIGHT An in-depth look at a specific area in the dungeon so you can better understand the types of threats to be found, as well as story prompts to start you off on a thrilling quest.

ENCOUNTER A dramatic passage and a critical choice to help inspire your own tales of action and adventure.

IRONSLAG
A Giant's Fortress

In the icy mountains north of the Silver Marches sits Ironslag, the fortress home of fire giant Duke Zalto.

Ironslag is not only a fortress but also a massive forge, where iron ore mined from within the mountain was once smelted and turned into axes, war hammers, and other mighty weapons. Abandoned thousands of years ago, it has been restored and reopened by Zalto, who seeks to build a colossal war machine, the Vonindod, that will allow him to wage an epic war and rise through the ranks of the giant lords.

Anyone who dares venture into Ironslag will face treacherous yakfolk (the yikaria, see page 82), formidable salamanders, powerful fire giants, and the terrible duke himself—plus his equally dangerous family. This perilous quest must be undertaken to prevent Zalto from laying waste to the world—and to plunder the many treasures hidden deep in the mountain!

Are you prepared to risk your life and enter the fire giant's forge?

OVERVIEW

The caverns that form the forges and halls of Ironslag are concealed behind a five-hundred-foot-tall cliff face. Visitors must navigate their way past a village of treacherous yakfolk and through a labyrinth of mines before finally reaching the foundry and the personal quarters of Duke Zalto and his family.

IMPORTANT PLACES

The sprawling complex of Ironslag is most quickly entered through fifty-foot-tall doors that can only be opened by a fire giant's magical command. Since they're unlikely to open the doors to adventuring parties, you'll have to take the long way around, through the yikaria village and into the mines.

Yikaria Village: A small and seemingly idyllic settlement, but its fields and mill are operated by slaves. The yikaria are very welcoming, because every stranger is another potential captive.

The Mines: This confusing maze of tunnels is linked together by rail tracks for iron carts. Salamanders, fearsome half-humanoid, half-serpentine fire elementals that thrive in molten heat, keep an eye on the dwarfs and gnomes forced to work here.

The Foundry: Ogres on the upper section of the foundry tip iron ore from the carts into the smelters, while fire giants below keep the smelters burning so the ore can be melted down to make weapons. The foundry is unbearably hot.

Assembly Hall: The main hall of the fortress, where the parts of the Vonindod hang suspended by chains from a ninety-foot-tall ceiling, and where Duke Zalto himself often sits at his throne, attended by his fearsome giant hounds, Narthor and Zerebor.

Adamantine Forge: A forge so hot it can melt and mold adamantine weapons and armor. The energy required to power it is very rare, so it has lain dormant for thousands of years.

THE FOUNDRY

The foundry at Ironslag is where iron ore mined from the mountain is melted down to be turned into weapons. The overseer of the foundry is Duke Zalto's spoiled and lazy teenage son, Zaltember. When adventurers encounter Zaltember, the young fire giant may be threatening to toss a prisoner into the molten iron below, simply for his own amusement.

Heroic adventurers may wish to step in and save the prisoner from a toasty fate, which would guarantee a battle with Zaltember high on the gantries above the smelting pit. Even those adventurers less inclined to risk their lives for a stranger may realize that taking Zaltember hostage could be an advantage as they travel deeper into Ironslag and risk coming face-to-face with his powerful father.

Of course, starting a fight in a foundry is very dangerous! Zaltember is immune to fire, and you probably aren't. Those fire giants below can't reach you up here, can they?

STORY PROMPTS

Dungeon Master: Capturing Zaltember will give adventurers leverage against Duke Zalto, but as soon as the fight begins, the fire giants will hurl burning lumps of molten iron at the heroes.

Player Character: Think about what you could gain from confronting Zaltember and saving the prisoner—but also consider what you might risk! Have you assessed every threat in the room?

INTO THE FIRE

Erun held the wound in her side and gritted her teeth. She was in bad shape after battling with the orcs, and might not survive another fight. Yet what choice did she have? Everything they feared had come to pass. Duke Zalto now possessed an iron flask that contained a primordial power, an elemental goddess who could relight the adamantine forge. With it, he could reconstruct the Vonindod colossus and begin his rampage of terror.

Erun's companion, Braelle, gestured for her to stay still as Braelle drew her own frost blade. One of Zalto's giant hounds was sniffing around while the fire giant slept on his throne, the iron bottle lightly gripped in his hand. Either Erun or Braelle would have to steal it from him.

It was supposed to be Erun. She had performed a bardic rite that would prevent both Zalto and his dogs from detecting her. Yet she might still be caught, especially in her wounded state.

"Let me go in your place," whispered Braelle. "I can step into the shadows and appear at Zalto's side, vanishing again before he can react."

It seemed like a solid plan, except for one thing. Although Braelle was Erun's friend, she was also a warlock, forever bound to a lord of darkness. If Braelle stole the primordial power, would she be tempted to claim it for her dark master?

What should Erun do? If she tries to grab the flask herself, the attempt might cost her life. Is she strong enough to fight back if Duke Zalto awakens? On the other hand, if she trusts Braelle to do it, what will she do if her companion betrays her and tries to steal the flask? The choice is up to you!

THE TEMPLE OF ELEMENTAL EVIL

A Shrine of Darkness

A terrible threat gathers in the north. Monsters are on the prowl, and raiders target isolated homesteads. Sinister strangers whisper of fires and floods that will lay waste to this peaceful land.

Four rival cults have arisen, each with their own tactics but a shared mission: To serve a mysterious force called the Elder Elemental Eye and wipe out civilization. The cults use their chosen element—earth, air, fire, or water—to wreak havoc as they strive to bring their Prince of Elemental Evil through a dimensional portal into this world before the others can do the same.

The scattered towns of this frontier land face a dire threat. If the forces of Elemental Evil can't be defeated, madness and destruction will spread through Slumber Hills and, if left unchecked, perhaps the entire realm. Will you stand against the cultists, their Elemental Princes, and the ultimate power of the Elder Elemental Eye?

OVERVIEW

The Temple of Elemental Evil is a sprawling complex of towers and keeps built around an underground bastion that houses four separate temples, one each dedicated to earth, air, fire, and water. Below all of these is the Temple of the Elder Elemental Eye, a meeting point for the cultists and the center of Elemental Evil.

IMPORTANT PLACES

The quiet town of Red Larch provides an idyllic entry point to Slumber Hills, where the four cults have built their strongholds. An outer ring of aboveground structures surrounds the underground temples, allowing the cultists to keep watch and guard against intruders. Those who are able to fight their way past these outer defenses will find themselves in an underground fortress divided into four separate temples, one for each element.

Temple of Black Earth: Worshipping the implacable strength of elemental earth, the Cult of the Black Earth seeks to destroy civilizations with landslides, earthquakes, and sinkholes. They are the most defense-minded of the four cults, and their heavily guarded temple reflects this fact. They are led by a medusa named Marlos Urnrayle, who wields Ironfang, a war pick infused with the power of Ogrémoch, the Prince of Evil Earth.

Temple of Crushing Wave: The Cult of the Crushing Wave is devoted to the awesome power of water, building their temple around a large underground spring called the Dark Stream. Cultists use surging tides, flooding rivers, and the rock-crushing power of glaciers to defeat their enemies. Their prophet is Gar Shatterkeel, a former sailor who carries Drown, a trident imbued with the essence of Olhydra, the Princess of Evil Water.

Temple of Eternal Flame: The destructive power of fire in all its manifestations inspires the Cult of the Eternal Flame, who built their temple around an underground lava pool. Hot-tempered and violent, they want to burn away the civilized world with volcanic eruptions, forest fires, heat waves, and droughts. They are led by Vanifer, an ambitious tiefling who carries the dagger Tinderstrike, which is infused with the power of Imix, the Prince of Evil Fire.

Temple of Howling Hatred: Raging storms and violent winds have earned the devotion of the Cult of the Howling Hatred, whose temple is built around an enormous cavern that channels the forces of air to attack intruders. Illusionists and spies, these cultists prefer to strike from the shadows rather than engage in open battle. Aerisi Kalinoth, a willowy moon elf, is their prophet. She bears the spear Windvane, which channels the power of Yan-C-Bin, the Prince of Evil Air.

CAVERN OF THE LOST CROWN

As soon as anyone touches the crowned helmet within this former dwarven stronghold, the ghost of a treasure hunter named Reulek appears. He uses a horrifying magical scream to try and frighten away adventurers, warning, "Beware thieves! Even in death, the dwarves of Besilmer guard their fabled treasure!"

These words summon the spirits of four dwarven warriors, who attack all living creatures in the cavern. If you manage to defeat the ghosts, you can speak with Reulek, who was killed by the spirits in this cavern as he attempted to steal the crown.

Reulek's ghost believes he is now bound to the relic, trapping him for eternity. He asks you to help him by returning the lost crown to the tomb of the last king of Besilmer. In exchange, he can provide valuable information about the cultists, which will help in your quest.

STORY PROMPTS

Dungeon Master: Can Reulek be trusted, or will he betray the adventuring party? What happens if the party refuses to help?

Player Character: Is the information that Reulek offers worth the risk of helping him by returning the crown? What is the best choice in this situation—let him suffer the punishment for his theft, or help free his soul from this magic curse?

GARGOYLE GUARDIANS

After defeating the earth cultists at Sacred Stone Monastery, Redclay and her companion, the wizard Inowyn, tracked the fleeing survivors to this vast chasm. Somewhere beyond the stone bridge, Marlos Urnrayle, the Prophet of Evil Earth, carried out his destructive plans.

"I'll take the one on the bridge," Redclay said, pointing her sword toward the two gargoyles who guarded the trestle. "You focus on the flyer."

As Redclay prepared to attack, Inowyn whispered a quick warning. "Wait! Do you see it? There, in the shadows?"

Redclay followed the half-elf's gesture toward the distant rocks, where she spotted the faint, craggy outline of a third gargoyle. While she was grateful for Inowyn's keen perception, she also realized their chances of success were now much worse.

"We still have those cultist robes we found at Sacred Stone," Inowyn said. "Maybe we should try sneaking past them?"

Redclay considered the options and frowned. A fight at the entrance would draw attention that they didn't want, and perhaps even give Marlos a chance to flee. On the other hand, if they tried to infiltrate by pretending to be cultists and failed, they'd lose the element of surprise and almost certainly be captured, making their quest even more difficult.

Should Redclay and Inowyn attempt a surprise attack on the gargoyles, risking their whole mission if the battle is noisy enough to alert the Temple to their presence? Would they be better off trying to sneak their way inside disguised as cultists—and what happens if their ruse fails? The choice is yours!

THE SEA GHOST

A Pirate Ship

The *Sea Ghost* is not a famous ship. You won't have heard of it, you wouldn't recognize it, and, if you're lucky, you'll never encounter it. As its name suggests, this "ghost" means to pass quietly through the night and leave little trace behind. If you *do* see this specter, you might be marked next for the grave.

The *Sea Ghost* is a smuggling ship crewed by pirates, though it also keeps a few secrets beneath its decks and among the barrels and crates of stolen goods and contraband.

The captain is a mean-spirited swashbuckler by the name of Sigurd Snake Eyes, and he's been using the *Sea Ghost* to smuggle goods in and out of the sleepy town of Saltmarsh for years.

The good people of Saltmarsh have had enough of this criminal tricking their town and stealing their treasure. Someone needs to board the *Sea Ghost* under cover of night and put an end to these pirates and their wicked ways.

OVERVIEW

The *Sea Ghost* is a single-sail ship, ninety feet long from prow to stern and twenty-six feet across at its widest point. Its main deck sits about nine feet above the waterline, with cabins at fore and aft. The ship is made largely of wood, though every part is slick with saltwater.

IMPORTANT PLACES

To board the *Sea Ghost*, you first must wait for it to come to you. That means setting up a watch on the shores of Saltmarsh until the smuggling ship makes its next visit and then rowing out to meet it. Adventurers face a choice between sneaking aboard from the seaward side of the ship while the crew is busy signaling the shore, or bluffing the smugglers into lowering a rope ladder.

Decks: If the alarm is raised upon boarding the *Sea Ghost*, adventurers will likely face an all-out battle on the slippery decks of the ship. Mind your feet!

Cabins and Galley: Beneath the raised forecastle and poop deck at the fore and aft of the ship are some of the ship's most important rooms, including the captain's cabin, the galley, and a cabin where some unexpected guests are staying—a trio of fierce and terrible lizardfolk, reptilian humanoids who prefer to settle in marshy swamps.

Cargo Hold: Below the main deck are the crew's quarters and the cargo hold. The hold contains most of the contraband that the ship is smuggling, though some rare treasures may lurk elsewhere on board.

The Bilge: You never know where smugglers might stash their treasure. Maybe even in the space between the lower deck and the hull? Or maybe the only things lurking down here are flesh-burrowing rot grubs?

Crow's Nest: Forty feet above the deck and accessible only by rope ladder is a lookout point at the top of the ship's mast. Adventurers who lack caution may get a nasty surprise when one of the smugglers starts raining arrows down on their heads!

THE MAIN DECK

The main deck of the *Sea Ghost* presents the most obvious opportunity for an open battle between adventurers and pirates. There's a wide slippery wooden floor, ropes from which to swing, and barrels to hurl, and it provides you with the chance to toss people overboard! It's the perfect place for a swashbuckling sword fight, and perhaps the only place on the ship where long-distance attacks will be effective.

However, there are also several cabins that open directly onto the deck, and adventurers don't know what lurks behind those doors. There may be vast treasures—or reinforcements.

Will your adventure aboard the *Sea Ghost* involve sneaking stealthily from room to room, or will it be an all-out brawl beneath the moonlight?

STORY PROMPTS

Dungeon Master: You know who is on this ship, but your adventurers do not. When is the best time to surprise them with an attack by lizardfolk?

Player Character: What's the best way to deal with the enemies in front of you before someone raises the alarm and brings other foes to the deck?

THE SECRET IN THE WALLS

Avaron figured it would be easy enough. While his fellow adventurers fought the pirates on the deck above, he would sneak below and pick through the cabins for the best treasures the *Sea Ghost* had to offer.

No one would have ever known, if he hadn't bumped a chair in the darkness. The noise brought the ship's conjurer to investigate, and Avaron was forced to retreat into the nearest empty cabin—only it wasn't empty after all.

Following the scratching noises from behind the wall, Avaron quickly found a secret panel leading to a hidden cell. Inside was a young sea elf blinking against the dim light, with chains binding his wrists and ankles.

Whoever this sea elf was, he was no friend of the pirates. Avaron could pick the elf's locks easily, maybe gaining an ally against the pirates when they tried to escape. Although looking at the state of him, the elf would probably need Avaron's last healing potion before he'd be any use in a fight.

Should Avaron trust the captured elf and hope they can battle the pirates together? Or would he have a better chance on his own? What will Avaron do if the elf turns out to be secretly in league with the pirates—or part of a plan to help the lizardfolk take over the ship, ruining Avaron's plans to make off with the pirate's stolen treasure? It's up to you to decide!

RAVENLOFT
A Vampire's Castle

In Barovia, a place of perpetual night, stands a terrifying castle that protects and imprisons the lord of this land. The citadel is called Ravenloft, and its owner is a powerful magic-wielding vampire named Strahd Von Zarovich.

Ravenloft is an opulent old castle adorned with gothic finery. It's protected by undead creatures, including skeletons, ghosts, werewolves, and, of course, vampire spawn. Its halls are dim and filled with all manners of curses and traps to ensnare any who dare trespass upon the count's property. Beneath the stronghold are burial chambers and prisons littered with old relics and deranged unliving monstrosities.

For as long as Count Strahd has been cursed with undead might, the sun has not risen in Barovia, and it will stay that way until a group of heroes finds the courage within themselves to fight back against the darkness and stop his reign of terror.

Do you dare venture into Ravenloft's frightening halls and twisting crypts?

OVERVIEW

Castle Ravenloft is a massive stone-built structure filled with secrets and danger. Its highest tower stands three hundred sixty feet tall, looming over the Barovian countryside, a constant reminder of Strahd's incredible power and influence.

IMPORTANT PLACES

Castle Ravenloft is surrounded by fifty-foot-wide chasms on all sides that plummet into eerie fog below. The drawbridge, normally closed unless the count is expecting visitors, is the only safe non-magical way across. Strahd leaves his gates and doors unlocked, confident that anyone foolish enough to enter will either be destroyed by his many minions, or, in rare cases, survive long enough to earn his personal attention.

Dining Hall: A massive chamber lit by three magnificent crystal chandeliers. A long, heavy table covered with fine satin cloth sits at the center of this room and a floor-to-ceiling pipe organ stands against the far wall.

Chapel: Once a holy place, the chapel was spoiled and left in disarray by Strahd's curse.

The Heart of Sorrow: A ten-foot-diameter glowing red crystal floating within one of the castle towers. This strange, magical formation absorbs pain inflicted on its vampiric master, an added level of protection that Strahd uses to survive against any foe foolish enough to attack him.

Hall of Heroes: A room of ten stone statues depicting Strahd's ancestors. Their spirits may provide important answers about the vampire's past and his weaknesses.

Catacombs: Forty crypts, some simple and unmarked, others ornate and covered with carvings and dedications, are organized in rows beneath the castle. Each one may contain a corpse, a creature, or hidden treasures.

Strahd's Tomb: Only the bravest and most well-prepared adventurers will be able to find Strahd's resting place and fight him in his own domain. Failure means death and then returning to life as one of the count's many vampiric servants.

THE BRAZIER ROOM

Beneath Castle Ravenloft, you'll find many different vaults—crypts, prisons, an armory, and a torture chamber. Among them is a strange room that provides a magical shortcut to any destination— or to a deadly demise for those who disturb its furnishings.

A stone brazier burns in the center of the room, but its tall white flame produces no heat. Around it are seven spheres made of tinted glass, each a different color. Above it hangs a large wood-framed hourglass, with glowing text written around the base.

> Cast a stone into the fire: Violet leads to the mountain spire
> Orange to the castle's peak / Red if lore is what you seek
> Green to where the coffins hide / Indigo to the master's bride
> Blue to ancient magic's womb / Yellow to the master's tomb

If you cast a colored sphere into the white flame, the fire changes hue to match and the hourglass's sand begins to drain. Touching the colored flame doesn't burn; instead, it magically transports you to a different part of the castle or elsewhere within the land of Barovia. After thirty seconds, the sand runs out, the fire changes back to white, and the glass sphere reappears, resetting the magic to be used again.

Two enchanted iron golems guard this space. If triggered, they attack all intruders with poison gas and crushing blows from their hooves and armor.

STORY PROMPTS

Dungeon Master: What brings the iron golems to life and makes them attack? Where will the brazier send your adventuring party—somewhere safe, or into greater danger?

Player Character: Will you use the power of the white flame to transport yourself to somewhere unknown?

SHOWDOWN WITH COUNT STRAHD

Ezmerelda averted her eyes and gasped as magic fire engulfed the hallway in an explosion of heat that seared her lungs. Almost as soon as the fire erupted, it stopped; Victor collapsed in pain, his battered plate armor smoking and charred.

Strahd chuckled as the last wisps of flame rippled from his hand. "All who oppose the Master of Ravenloft learn their place. You should feel honored that I chose to dispose of you personally instead of leaving it to my faithful followers."

Ezmerelda held aloft her silver-plated shortsword and prepared to attack Strahd again. She could tell for all the count's bravado, the vampire was wounded and the potent spell had used up his strength. This could be her chance to finally end the vampire's reign of terror upon the people of Barovia.

Strahd sensed her resolve and was in no rush to test his might against hers. Before Ezmerelda could strike, the master vampire began turning to mist. As his features shimmered and diffused, he cackled, "You know where my crypt lies, foolish child. Follow me there and battle to your last breath, or save your friend and live to fight another day. . . ."

Should Ezmerelda stay with Victor and carry him to safety, saving his life? Or should she follow Strahd back to his coffin, taking this rare chance to strike while the count is injured—an opportunity that might not come again? It's up to you!

CHULT
An Island of Dinosaurs

Chult is a wild and beautiful island where blue waves lap against golden beaches, and wide rivers wend lazily through lush, green forests. On first glimpse, it may seem like a paradise. But you won't have to travel far into its verdant interior to have that illusion shattered.

The island is a dangerous and deadly place where almost everything seems designed to kill you, from carnivorous plants to militant frogs, hidden pit traps to angry gods. Chult's most notorious inhabitants include people-eating dinosaurs, brain-devouring zombies, and an undead spellcaster named Acererak. (And those are just the threats that have been reported!) Much of the island remains unexplored by outsiders—or, more accurately, many explorers have ventured forth and never come back.

Even still, Chult is a land of treasure where rich civilizations have risen and fallen, and artifacts of great power have disappeared. Merchants from around the world have tried to exploit the island's natural wealth but failed. For many who delve deep into the tropics of Chult, it is a paradise. For others, it is their tomb.

OVERVIEW

Chult is a vast tropical island that calls to explorers, many of whom long to conquer its untamed forests and discover its secrets. Largely cut off from the world by the formidable mountains that line its coast, Chult harbors many mysteries, and has infinite ways to keep them hidden.

IMPORTANT PLACES

To reach Chult, you'll need to sail the Sea of Broken Dreams and land at Port Nyanzaru, the island's only modern city. You can get information and supplies from local merchants—and get your pocket picked by the local thieves' guild, if you're not careful. From Port Nyanzaru, you can explore the island's many forts, mines, and temples, and what remains of the civilizations that once thrived here.

Hrakhamar: A dwarven forge that was abandoned after being flooded by volcanic magma. Firenewts have since taken over the caverns. The magma has receded, and now dwarves want to reclaim it.

Jahaka Anchorage: A sea cave so large that ships can find safe shelter within its walls. The cave offers easy access to the jungle, but the merchants that use it are not always welcoming to strangers. (Rumor has it they're not entirely legitimate traders.)

Nangalore: Ornate and palatial terraced gardens that long ago fell into disrepair, though the queen they were built to honor is said to still lurk among the ruins, transformed by grief and dark magic into something terrible!

Omu: Chult's great lost city, once known for its wealth and splendor, has been reclaimed by the jungle. Twisted vines have consumed its famous shrines, and dinosaurs roam its streets.

Fane of the Night Serpent: The yuan-ti, a tribe of devious snakepeople, are the dominant force in fallen Omu. They reside in this expansive temple beneath the city's former palace.

Tomb of the Nine Gods: Omu was once ruled by nine trickster gods, who were destroyed many centuries ago. In their place has risen the archlich Acererak, who transforms the souls of fallen heroes into fuel for his evil magic.

DUNGRUNGLUNG

If your travels through the jungles of Chult bring you to Dungrunglung, a settlement of the aggressive and territorial froglike grungs, you may find yourself entangled in a very strange adventure. The vain and short-tempered grung king, Groak, wants to conduct a ritual to summon the goddess Nangnang to be his bride. The high priestess, Krr'ook, fears for her life if the ceremony fails, and she believes that outsiders may be able to help her fool the king.

Grungs may not look like much, but their numbers, agility, and sheer ferocity make them dangerous, and you're unlikely to pass through their territory without getting in trouble. You can distract and flatter King Groak for a time, but your best hope of surviving an encounter with the grungs may be to make an alliance with Krr'ook to aid in her schemes.

STORY PROMPTS

Dungeon Master: How can you place your adventurers at Groak's mercy, so that an alliance with Krr'ook is their only way out?

Player Character: How would you fool a mad king into believing that his goddess has manifested in front of him?

THE SCHEMES OF RAS NSI

In service to his merciful goddess, young half-orc Kez ventured into the fallen city of Omu, hoping to end the terror of Ras Nsi, a fellow paladin corrupted by a dark god and returned from death as a serpentine necromancer. He had heard tell of such abominations, deathless beasts summoned back to life in decay and wickedness, and expected a brutal fight.

He did not expect a monkey. A vicious little screeching, flying monkey that tore at him with its tiny hands and feet.

Kez tried to ignore the little beast as he reached for his sacred medallion—a gift from his goddess—which he believed could send Ras Nsi to oblivion. It contained a spell for destroying the undead, one powerful enough to vanquish even this villain.

But then, the medallion was gone. Kez panicked as the monkey flew down the dank corridor with the amulet gripped in its paws.

Kez had sworn an oath that he would end Ras Nsi's reign of terror this night. Now fear and doubt crept into his soul. Could he accomplish his destiny without his goddess's blessing?

Should Kez chase after his stolen medallion, knowing that Ras Nsi might escape—and how will he get it back from the tricky flying monkey if he chooses this path? Or should he confront Ras Nsi directly, hoping to prevail even without his powerful holy weapon? The choice is yours!

UNDERMOUNTAIN
Grand Dungeon of the Mad Mage

Undermountain is the largest, deepest dungeon of them all. Burrowing through and under Mount Waterdeep are miles upon miles of tunnels, ranging from wide, well-carved passageways to narrow cracks roughly cut from raw rock.

All this is the work of the Mad Mage, Halaster Blackcloak, a wizard who has spent the last thousand years building this massive and dangerous dungeon. He has stocked it with terrifying creatures from across the lands, ensuring his privacy as he continues his eccentric eldritch experiments deep underground.

Treasure and glory await any adventurers brave enough to enter the sprawling labyrinth of Undermountain, but so do mighty monsters, terrifying traps, and the risk of madness. Something strange and rotten lies at the heart of Undermountain, a mysterious force that twists the minds of all who approach.

Are you ready to risk your sanity to plunder the rewards that await below?

OVERVIEW

Undermountain is a complex dungeon containing hundreds of miles of passageways and rooms, all buried beneath enormous Mount Waterdeep. At its core resides the Mad Mage, a powerful wizard obsessed with expanding both his dungeon and his magical knowledge.

IMPORTANT PLACES

The only access point to Undermountain is through the Yawning Portal, a warm and friendly inn built above the ruins of the Mad Mage's original wizard tower. Once inside, explorers will face a seemingly endless maze of hallways and rooms, each layer built in a different style and harboring its own unique dangers.

Arcane Chambers: The ruins of the Mad Mage's original dwelling, this area has been overtaken by goblins who run a market for denizens of Undermountain. It is a huge hall with sixty-foot-high ceilings supported by two rows of stone pillars.

Caverns of Ooze: A series of naturally formed tunnels and chambers carved out by the slow passage of primordial slime. This is the dwelling place for a huge gray ooze and two intelligent black puddings, among other nasty creatures.

Crystal Labyrinth: This glittering area is carved from multihued crystal and features several large caverns with soaring ceilings studded with sparkling stalactites.

Slitherswamp: Muck-filled caverns and damp, dangerous shrubbery make up this watery level, which is filled with humidity, buzzing insects, and the remains of an evil serpent cult.

Trobriand's Graveyard: Known as the Metal Mage, Trobriand specialized in creating magical constructs from steel and iron. Eventually he transferred his own consciousness into one of his bizarre creations. This area is filled with metallic monstrosities and voracious rust monsters.

The Mad Mage's Lair: The residence of Halaster Blackcloak, this area features an upside-down library, a room filled with talking heads in jars, an animated hallway that never stops moving, and a portal that leads to Halaster's Tower, a three-story spire that crosses over into another dimension.

THE DRAGON'S HATCHERY

Undermountain is home to a dizzying array of creatures, but even among this menagerie, the red dragon Ashtyrranthor and her six children make an impression. The dragon family resides in a series of majestic tunnels beneath the Crystal Labyrinth, heated by lava pools and protected by magical illusions.

The highlight of these chambers is a hatchery, where a dragon egg rests gently in the center of the lava pool. Many a magical scholar would pay handsomely for such a treasure, leaving your party with quite a dilemma. You could try to steal the egg, either for your own magical research or to sell to a wealthy patron. You could destroy it, preventing the birth of a dangerous dragon. Or you could leave it be, knowing that dragons are fiercely protective of their offspring.

Whatever you decide, you'll have to do it quickly—within this part of the dragon's lair, the temperature, at 120 degrees Fahrenheit, is too high for non-dragons to handle for more than an hour. Make sure your party comes to a decision quietly as well. Loud noises in the hatchery will surely draw the attention of Ashtyrranthor!

STORY PROMPTS

Dungeon Master: Is the dragon egg real, or only a clever fake like the other illusion rooms in the lair?

Player Character: Will you risk stealing the dragon egg, or continue exploring in hopes of finding better treasure? If you try to reach the egg, what techniques can you use to avoid scorching yourself on the lava?

BLACKCLOAK'S BARGAIN

Urnath grunted as another of the metallic insects crunched beneath her war hammer. Before she could savor the victory, her companion, Puknik, shouted a warning, directing her attention toward the ceiling. Moments ago there had only been twisted metal and the angry buzz of the mechanical wasps, but now a grinning man in elegant wizard robes hovered in the same spot.

"The Mad Mage!" cried Puknik, before unleashing a *magic missile* spell. The glowing arrows passed harmlessly through the illusion. "Though not in the flesh. . . ."

"Of course not, you foolish spell-slinger," replied Halaster Blackcloak with a giggle. "I have a task for you. A trifle, really. Clear out these metal creations, leftovers from my former apprentice, Trobriand, and I'll reward you handsomely. A magical hammer for you, and a scroll containing one of my custom spells for your friend. What say you?"

The companions traded a solemn glance. Who knew how many of these creatures there were, and how much time it would take from their real quest, rescuing a kidnapped nobleman from his goblin captors. But, if they failed to accept this new task, the Mad Mage's anger would likely turn against them, making their original mission even more difficult, if not impossible. Unable to speak freely in front of Blackcloak, Urnath and Puknik must decide quickly.

Should they accept this new quest, or continue on their original mission? What are the odds that Blackcloak will keep his promise if they succeed? Or will the Mad Mage change his mind and betray them at a crucial moment? Is there a way to accomplish both quests in the limited time available? Where the story goes is up to you!

DUNGEON BESTIARY

Dungeons are fascinating and fearsome, filled with danger and despair, traps and treasures. Some are abandoned strongholds from ancient times, while others are natural caves or lairs carved out by foul beasts. Most have been in use for centuries, building up layers of enchantment and distinctive features that give birth to entirely new types of monsters.

The hidden nooks of a dungeon are fertile breeding ground for all manner of fungi, vermin, and scavengers. Once-normal beasts are sometimes warped by living underground for generations, evolving in unusual and deadly ways. Spellcasters create magical servants and powerful guardians who persist in their tasks long after their creator has moved on or passed away.

Designed to thrive in harsh and violent environments, these creatures are ruthless and lethal. Whatever form they take, beasts bred for dungeon life are among the deadliest a hero will ever face.

DANGER LEVELS

Each monster profile includes a number indicating the danger level of that creature, with a **0** being harmless, a **1** as a reasonable threat for a beginning adventurer, and building up from there. A **5** is incredibly dangerous and requires an experienced group of adventurers to possibly defeat it. There are some **epic** creatures more powerful than a mere number can define. Such terrors can only be fought by legendary heroes armed with the most powerful magic weapons and spells imaginable.

BASILISK

TRAINING A BASILISK Basilisk eggs are a rare treasure because a basilisk raised from an egg can be trained to obey its master! As you might imagine, basilisks make excellent—if nasty—"guard dogs."

SIZE Basilisks are large reptilian creatures with bodies that grow to about six feet in length, and tails that can grow just as long, making them, overall, about the size of a large Komodo dragon.

Basilisks are terrifying predators due to the unique way they snare their prey. Their cold gaze has the power of petrification, which means they can turn flesh to stone. Once their prey is transformed, a basilisk can crush the resulting statue in its formidable jaws, with the stone turning back into meat as the basilisk swallows. It's a terrible way to meet your fate!

Encountering a basilisk does not mean instant death. If you're tough enough, you might survive the initial glance. However, the moment the effect takes hold, only the right spell or an antidote can save you.

Some alchemists can make basilisk antidote from the creature's guts; but to do that, you need to hunt a basilisk—and you don't want to hunt a basilisk without the antidote handy, so you can see the conundrum.

LAIR Basilisks prefer sheltered lairs in warm climates, such as caves in a dry rocky desert or a burrow in a tropical forest. One easy way to tell if a basilisk has made a home nearby is to look for the remains of its prey in the form of shattered statues.

DO THIS

Polish your shield or sword. A reflective metal surface can sometimes trick a basilisk into attacking itself.

Run! Basilisks are not very fast, because they don't need to be.

DON'T DO THIS

Don't look directly at a basilisk. It needs only one glance to start turning you to stone.

Don't ignore statues. Ruined statues can indicate a nearby basilisk—especially statues of unusual subjects, standing in strange poses or looking afraid.

FLAMESKULL

SPECIAL POWERS

SPELLCASTING
Flameskulls retain some magical powers, and can cast some lower-level spells such as *magic missile*, *shield*, *flaming sphere*, and *fireball*.

REJUVENATION
When destroyed, a flameskull can reassemble itself to full health within one hour, unless holy water is sprinkled on the remains to dispel its magic.

SIZE A flameskull is the size of a normal skull for the humanoid from which it was created, except surrounded by a half-foot of crackling flames.

These magical guardians can only be created from the skulls of dead wizards, and make excellent protectors for a spellcaster's secrets. Perpetually burning with bright-green flame, flameskulls drift and cackle through their assigned patrols, having been driven mad by the ritual that made them.

Flameskulls will attack intruders on sight, spitting fire rays from their mouths. Flameskulls can also cast a spell called *mage hand*, which lets them open doors and move small objects even though they no longer have hands of their own. Halaster Blackcloak, the Mad Mage of Undermountain, has a number of flameskulls that he uses to guard his secrets and spy on those who enter his dungeon.

LAIR Most flameskulls will be found within the lairs of their creators, powerful spellcasters who may reside in a wizard tower, an underground dungeon, or a vast ancient library. They may also be found within the ruins where a spellcaster once lived, carrying out their ghostly routines.

DO THIS	DON'T DO THIS
Disperse your party. You'll be harder for a flameskull to hit with a fireball if you split up, instead of bunching together.	**Don't rely on magic to win.** Flameskulls have magic resistance, so it's easier to defeat one with physical weapons.
Splash a dead flameskull with holy water. Otherwise, the creature will come back to life in one hour.	**Don't try to reason with it.** Flameskulls remember almost nothing from their former lives, except for the magic spells that they can still cast.

GIBBERING MOUTHER

1

SPECIAL POWERS

BLINDING SPITTLE

The mouther spits a chemical glob up to fifteen feet, which explodes on impact to release a bright flash that temporarily blinds all creatures within a five-foot radius.

GIBBERING

The manic babbling of a gibbering mouther can paralyze a target with fear, making them unable to escape as the creature moves closer. This effect impacts all adventurers within twenty feet.

SIZE A gibbering mouther is about the height of a professional basketball player and as wide at the bottom as a dining room table. Their elastic flesh does not have a fixed shape, but instead stretches and squishes as the creature moves.

Of all the monsters animated by evil sorcery, the gibbering mouther may be the most nightmarish. These foul creatures are covered with the eyes, mouths, and melting flesh of their former victims. They shamble and ooze through dungeons in search of their next prey, driven mad by the wicked magic that animates them. The very ground dissolves around them as they move, creating a mudlike surface that is difficult to escape.

Endlessly hungry, gibbering mouthers cannot contain their excitement if they sense prey is nearby. Their multiple mouths begin to mumble and chatter, each with its own unique voice. This cacophony can drive anyone who hears it temporarily mad. Some may flee in panic, while others are transfixed to the spot, unable to move as the gibbering mouther slowly flows over them and begins dissolving their flesh.

LAIR Gibbering mouthers are created by evil magic and often found in the dungeons of powerful, villainous spellcasters. They move slowly across solid ground but can swim easily through water, quicksand, and mud, making them adaptable to a variety of dungeon environments.

DO THIS

Cover your ears. If you can't hear the gibbering mouther, it can't leave you frozen in fear.

Rescue your pals. Even if a party member is enveloped by a gibbering mouther, you still have a chance to rescue them—at least, until you see a pair of familiar eyes pop up on the creature's body!

DON'T DO THIS

Don't get too close. The ground around a gibbering mouther is uneven and perilous. Distance attacks are your safest bet.

Don't ignore its teeth. The noises from all those mouths can be dangerous, but don't forget that numerous mouths also means many, many sharp teeth.

GRUNG

SPECIAL POWERS

STANDING LEAP
From a standing position, grungs can instantly leap up to fifteen feet in the air or twenty-five feet ahead of their former positions, allowing them to quickly strike opponents during combat.

POISON EXCRETION
All grungs excrete a dangerous poison that is harmless to them but nasty to any other type of creature.

SIZE Even the tallest grung is too short to reach the countertop in a human kitchen (maybe that's why they're so grumpy!). They have stocky bodies with thin legs, but their sticky toepads give them excellent balance.

Grungs are small, and to some they may appear cute, but they're certainly not harmless. These brightly colored froglike humanoids should never be underestimated. In fact, they can hurt you without even trying, thanks to the poisonous residue that seeps naturally from their skin. Just touching a Grung is enough to do serious damage!

Grungs are also dangerous because they're belligerent, bad-tempered, and more than happy to cause trouble. They're proudly defensive of their territory and can leap up to twenty-five feet in a single bound, appearing as if out of nowhere with their weapons drawn once they land. Some grungs can also make a sound that briefly stuns or mesmerizes their foes.

Grungs live in a strictly divided society, with each grung taking on the color of their assigned social role as they grow older. Green grungs are fighters and workers, blue grungs are artisans and homemakers, purple grungs are administrators, red grungs are scholars, orange grungs are elite warriors, and gold grungs are the ruling class.

LAIR Most grungs live on the Isle of Chult, making their homes in the festering swamps. They need to be close to water at all times, and prefer shady locations with lots of plant cover.

DO THIS

Stay dry. Grungs prefer wet terrain, but all that dampness will have a negative effect on your weapons and other gear.

Offer to help. Grungs want to protect their territory. If you can demonstrate you're not a threat, and offer to help them against someone who is, they might listen.

DON'T DO THIS

Don't touch. The poison on grung skin can take effect in an instant.

Don't be fooled by their size. Grungs may look tiny, but they pack a punch that hits harder than you'd expect.

IRON GOLEM

4

SPECIAL POWERS

FIRE ABSORPTION
Created in the blazing heat of a forge, iron golems are not only immune to fire damage, they can actually heal when attacked by flames!

POISONOUS BREATH
Iron golems exhale a fifteen-foot cone of poison gas, which damages anyone exposed to the noxious fumes.

SIZE Iron golems can be created in any size, from eight to sixteen feet tall, depending on how much raw material their creator has on hand. Most range in height from the top of a volleyball net to the bottom of a basketball hoop.

An iron golem is a living statue made of heavy metal. Every step it takes shakes the ground beneath its feet and its fists hit like giant hammers, crushing whatever gets in the way.

Golems are created using powerful magic, binding a spirit to an inanimate object. Iron golems are the most powerful, as their bodies are nearly impervious to harm. They can spout deadly poison gas and smash almost anything standing in their way. These unstoppable juggernauts exist only to do the bidding of their creators, protecting and attacking mindlessly as ordered.

LAIR As constructs who must obey all orders they are given, golems do not have a natural lair. They can often be found guarding the residence or workshop of the spellcaster who created them. Since they do not age, iron golems can be found in abandoned ruins, still obeying the orders of a creator who has long since died and gone to dust.

DO THIS

Break out the magic. Regular weapons won't even scratch an iron golem. You'll need magic to get through their iron shell.

Stay clear of poison gas. Once you see the golem start to spew its cloud of deadly smoke, move back and try to attack it from behind.

DON'T DO THIS

Don't get underfoot. If you get too close, an iron golem can smash you beneath its huge stomping feet.

Don't use fire. Heating the metal of an iron golem heals the creature instead of hurting it.

LIZARDFOLK

1

SPECIAL POWERS

MULTI-ATTACK
Highly trained warriors, lizardfolk can make two attacks each round, choosing between their sharp bites, heavy clubs, thrown javelins, and spiked shields to damage their enemies.

BREATH HOLDING
Lizardfolk can go without breathing for up to 15 minutes, enabling them to fight underwater and resist attack by poison gas.

SIZE Lizardfolk are slightly taller than humans, with broad torsos and thick tails that give them extra bulk. Imagine a bodybuilder with a huge reptile tail and you're on the right track.

Lizardfolk are a race of reptilian humanoids who generally keep to their own society, living in simple tribal communes usually led by a sole chieftain. They prefer to settle in areas of marsh and swamp, and they often build their homes in dank caves, from which they set out on their daily hunts.

Though lizardfolk can eat almost anything, they have a strong preference for meat, and by some reports they especially enjoy human flesh. Anyone venturing into lizardfolk territory could find themselves marked as prey.

Larger than humans, and with tough scaly hides, lizardfolk are intimidating creatures, and unwary travelers should make note of their snapping teeth and razor-sharp claws. Though lizardfolk hunt and fight with weapons, they're still very dangerous when unarmed!

LAIR Lizardfolk can be found in swamps and jungles, where they stake out hunting grounds with camouflaged scouts who keep watch for any intruders. These fiercely territorial creatures do not appreciate visitors, although they may throw a feast to celebrate your arrival—you'll be the main dish, however.

DO THIS

Watch the teeth. Don't be so distracted by a lizardfolk's weapon attack that you don't notice them lunging for a bite of your tantalizing flesh!

Stay stealthy. If you must cross through lizardfolk territory, do so quietly and carefully if you want to avoid a tough fight.

DON'T DO THIS

Don't get in their way. Lizardfolk are great hunters; if they're tracking prey, you don't want to give them a reason to switch focus!

Don't assume they're simple. Tribal communities often do things in ways that others are not used to, but that doesn't mean they're unsophisticated. Every community has its own systems and culture.

MIMIC

SPECIAL POWERS

SHAPECHANGE
Mimics can hide their true forms, appearing instead as a wide range of inanimate objects. This deception can't be detected so long as the mimic remains motionless. When killed, the creature reverts back to its true form.

ADHESION
Mimics give off a gooey substance that sticks both creatures and objects to its body. Any limb or weapon stuck to the creature can't be used to fight it, so you'll need to get unstuck quickly if you want to survive!

SIZE
Disguised, mimics are the average size of the object they are imitating, so about two feet tall for a chest to six feet tall for a door. They rarely shift entirely into their natural form, but when they do, they appear as a lumpy blob between three and five feet tall.

Not everything in a dungeon is what it appears to be. Mimics are shapeshifting predators that take the form of inanimate objects to lure in their prey (hint: that's you). In dungeons, mimics most often appear as doors or treasure chests, although they can take on many different shapes.

They can alter their appearance to look like wood, metal, stone, and other basic materials, making them indistinguishable from the original object they are copying. Once their prey gets close enough, the monsters spout pseudopods and attack. Mimics excrete a sticky substance when they change shape, which helps them hang on to both victims and the victims' weapons.

LAIR Mimics live and hunt alone, seeking out well-traveled spots within dungeons where they can be assured of a steady stream of prey. They sometimes share their lairs with other creatures, although their predatory instincts make them bad roommates.

DO THIS

Approach with caution. Don't let your excitement of possible treasure blind you to the risk that a tempting chest may represent.

Poke it with a stick. Using a quarterstaff or walking stick to prod at inanimate objects before touching them can help you avoid a mimic.

DON'T DO THIS

Don't focus on melee attacks. The sticky surfaces of mimics mean that swords and other melee weapons can become trapped on their skin, making it impossible to keep fighting. Try a ranged attack instead!

OOZE

SIZE Oozes range in size from five to fifteen square feet. Gray oozes tend to be smallest, while gelatinous cubes are often large enough to fill an average dungeon hallway.

Black Pudding

Gelatinous Cube

Gray Ooze

Ochre Jelly

Human

Oozes dwell in the darkness. These slimy creatures slither through dungeons in search of prey, swallowing up everything they find, before slowly dissolving it within their shambling forms. Drawn to movement and warmth, they are constantly seeking fresh victims. Death by ooze is deeply unpleasant, as it often takes several hours for the creature to gradually melt its victim's flesh. On the plus side, this slow dissolution can give a target the time needed to be rescued by their allies.

Oozes have no sense of tactics or self-preservation. They behave in predictable ways, moving toward possible prey and away from bright lights. Because oozes are not intelligent, smarter creatures can manipulate them into serving as unwitting allies, guarding important passageways or serving as traps for unwary adventurers. Since oozes' corrosive effects do not work on most metal, jewels, and magical items, an ooze's corpse can be a rich source of treasure for victorious adventurers.

LAIR Oozes are capable of making a home in any dark, dank dungeon space. They cluster in gloomy corners where they can slowly dissolve their victims without being disturbed, but can also be found shambling through busy (but unlit) hallways in search of fresh food.

DO THIS

Light your way. Oozes are sensitive to bright lights and will move away from dungeon areas that are highly illuminated.

Beware of clean floors. Most dungeons don't have maid service. If the ground is swept clean of all debris, the odds are good that an ooze has passed by recently.

DON'T DO THIS

Don't give up on a swallowed ally. Oozes take hours to fully digest their prey. Even if a party member is swallowed by one, you may still have time to rescue them.

Don't wait for nap time. These unnatural creatures don't require sleep, so it's hard to catch them off guard.

BLACK PUDDING

A black pudding appears as a heaving mass of sticky black sludge. It prefers dark passageways, where it can blend in with the shadows. Experienced adventurers know that a clean hallway is a warning that a black pudding has swept through recently.

SPECIAL POWERS

CORROSION
Black pudding dissolves flesh, wood, metal, and bone. Touching it with bare skin burns like acid, and non-magical weapons are damaged by contact.

AMORPHOUSNESS
The malleable body of a black pudding lets it squeeze through impossibly tiny gaps. Even an inch will do!

GELATINOUS CUBE

Gelatinous cubes travel through dungeon passages in silent, predictable patterns. They consume living flesh, but cannot dissolve bones or other materials. You can detect a well-fed cube by the bones and belongings of its recent victims, still suspended within the moving creature.

SPECIAL POWERS

ENGULFMENT
By moving into an individual's space, the gelatinous cube can engulf its target, completely surrounding it with ooze. Engulfed creatures are burned by the cube's acidic form and cannot breathe while inside.

TRANSPARENCY
A gelatinous cube is completely transparent, aside from any undigested remains from previous victims that it may contain. As a result, it is almost completely invisible when not moving.

GRAY OOZE

When still, gray ooze looks exactly like wet stone. This allows the ooze to blend perfectly with stone walls and floors, lying in wait for prey to pass. Only when it moves to attack does the gray ooze become visible, rising up like a liquid snake to strike at its intended victim. Like black pudding, gray ooze has corrosion and amorphousness powers.

OCHRE JELLY

1

These yellowish blobs slide under doors and through narrow cracks, and even crawl upside-down on the ceiling, in pursuit of food. They are just smart enough to avoid large groups, waiting for better odds before attacking. Like gelatinous cubes, ochre jelly can dissolve flesh but not bone, wood, metal, or other materials. They are immune to damage from lightning or sharp weapons.

ROPER

2

SPECIAL POWERS

GRAPPLING

Ropers can have up to six tendrils, which they use to grab their targets and pull them closer. Each tendril has hairlike protrusions that can penetrate a creature's skin and sap their strength, making escape even harder. If a tendril is cut off, the roper can regenerate a new one in its place.

SPIDER CLIMBING

Ropers can climb difficult surfaces with ease, including along walls and across ceilings. They move slowly but silently.

MULTI-ATTACK

A roper can make up to six attacks at once, including four tendril strikes, one bite, and one attempt to pull a target in close to them.

SIZE Ropers are typically between eight and sixteen feet long, about the size of a family car. They have up to six tendrils, a single eye, and dangerously sharp teeth.

Ropers are patient predators that mimic the rock protrusions of caves, pushing up from the ground or hanging down from above, waiting for prey to approach. Unlike real rocks, ropers can move (although slowly), sliding silently along until they are in the perfect position to attack. When still, ropers are indistinguishable from normal rocks.

When a roper attacks, its single eye opens and up to six tendrils lash out at the target. A wide mouth filled with jagged teeth snaps out to bite, while making terrible guttural sounds to intimidate prey. Ropers can digest almost anything, except platinum, gemstones, and magical items. Gruesome as it sounds, some adventurers have found great treasures by searching through a roper's stomach once it's dead!

LAIR Ropers are typically found in less-refined parts of a dungeon, such as natural caves or rough-hewn rooms. They can appear as either stalagmites, pushing up from the dungeon floor, or stalactites, hanging from above.

DO THIS

Attack with all you've got. Ropers may look like rock but they can be hurt by regular weapons. So stab, slash, and use magic to strike down these creatures as quick as you can.

Watch for moving rocks. Ropers will move into the best position before attacking; so when exploring caves, keep an eye out for rocks that change locations.

DON'T DO THIS

Don't relax (even after they're dead). Ropers make loud guttural noises while attacking, which can alert other creatures to investigate. Don't let your guard down too soon.

SEA ELF

SPECIAL POWERS

FRIEND OF THE SEA
Using gestures and sounds, sea elves can communicate simple ideas to ocean creatures, asking them to keep watch, retrieve small objects, or perform other simple tasks.

CHILD OF THE SEA
Sea elves can move quickly through water. They can breathe both air and water, moving at will between land and ocean environments.

SIZE Like their land-based cousins, sea elves are slightly slimmer and taller than humans. Their skin tone ranges from green to blue, and they have visible gills on their necks and chest.

Thousands of years ago, some members of the ancient race of elves turned their attention to the beauty of the sea and devoted their long lives to exploring its depths and understanding its varied mysteries. Through magical means, they developed the ability to live their entire lives underwater.

All elves share a love for nature, but sea elves have a special devotion to the sea. They make a point of befriending its many other inhabitants and exploring its murky shadows. Sea elves have learned secrets that no one on the shoreline may ever know!

Like all elves, sea elves can easily be friend or foe depending on the circumstances in which you encounter them. They tend to be reclusive, and the oceans are vast, so you may only ever meet a sea elf when some crisis forces them to the surface world.

LAIR As their name suggests, sea elves live beneath the ocean waves, usually in underwater caves or cities. They mainly reside in small hidden communities, which resonate with the beautifully eerie music unique to the sea elves.

DO THIS	DON'T DO THIS
Approach in peace. Sea elves specialize in ranged attacks. If they think you're approaching with bad intentions, you may end up on the wrong end of a trident!	**Don't try to swim away.** Sea elves are excellent and graceful swimmers and can breathe underwater. They'll catch up to you very quickly!
Look out for sea creatures. Sea elves can communicate in very simple ways with aquatic animals, so sea creatures that are behaving strangely may be acting as spies for the sea elves.	**Don't pollute the sea.** Sea elves care deeply about their home and do not take kindly to people who try to ruin it.

WATER ELEMENTAL MYRMIDON

SPECIAL POWERS

FREEZING STRIKE
This power adds a cold blast to normal trident attacks, doing extra damage and slowing down their target for a few seconds.

ELEMENTAL IMMUNITY
As elementals, myrmidons cannot be paralyzed, petrified, poisoned, or knocked over. They also take less damage from non-magical attacks, such as normal swords or arrows.

SIZE The size of a water elemental myrmidon is determined by the size of the magical plate mail into which it's bound. While giant-size myrmidons exist (and are terrifying), most are slightly larger than humans, although they can manipulate their watery form to appear taller.

Water elemental myrmidons are conjured by elemental power and shackled into specially created suits of plate mail armor by a complex magical ritual. They possess no memory of their former existence as free elementals bound to a specific water-filled location, such as a pool or a fountain, and must obey every command given by their creator.

Water elemental myrmidons carry magic three-pronged tridents that they can use to make melee attacks. They also have a freezing strike power that does additional cold damage when they land a hit with their trident.

LAIR As bound magical creatures, they live wherever their creator orders them to be, which is usually guarding an important location or valuable treasure. Most elementals must exist within or near to their element, but myrmidons are free from that restriction, since their plate mail armor serves as their personal lair.

DO THIS

Break out your magical attacks. Water elemental myrmidons are resistant to normal damage, so you'll need magical weapons and spells to win this fight.

Set them free. If you can break the spell that binds them to their armor, a free water elemental is likely to flee rather than keep fighting.

DON'T DO THIS

Don't try to poison them. Their watery bodies easily flush out any poisons, making them immune to such attacks.

Don't target their creator. The spell that binds a water elemental myrmidon to its armor won't break if you defeat the original spellcaster.

YIKARIA

SPECIAL POWERS

SKIN CRAWLING

Yikaria have the ability to take over someone else's body. Known as "skin crawling," this psychic attack allows them to control their victims' every action. Fortunately, the yikaria require at least an hour of constant physical contact to complete this process, so they can't take over one of your allies during a fight.

SIZE Yikarai resemble disgruntled yaks, if yaks stood on their two hind legs and wore primitive clothes. They're about as tall as an ostrich, but almost twice as heavy.

The yikaria, also known as yakfolk, are a race of hulking humanoids with faces, fur, and horns that resemble those of yaks. They live in remote hidden settlements that appear to visitors a lot like paradise due to the yikaria life of luxury and leisure.

In reality, yikaria culture is heartless and cruel, built on the backs of slaves. Any visitors who stumble into their enclaves are likely to find themselves in chains. By forcing others to do all their work, the yikaria are free to pursue their passion for dark magic and to dedicate themselves to the worship of a vile deity called the Forgotten God.

Among the dark powers the yikaria can tap into is an ability called "skin crawling," which allows them to take possession of the minds of other creatures by meditating for a short period while maintaining physical contact with their victim. Through this power, they can effectively turn an adventurer against their most trusted allies!

LAIR Yikaria prefer to live in somewhat remote areas, where there are few others to question the dark secret behind their seemingly idyllic communities. Their largest settlement is at Ironslag, where a yikaria village marks the main entrance to the mines, and a watermill powers the elevator that takes people into the forge below.

DO THIS

Keep out of sight. The safest way to deal with the yikaria is to never encounter them at all. When attacked, the yikaria often slaughter their slaves to prevent an uprising.

Stay awake. If you fall asleep in a yikaria enclave, you'll either end up a slave or be possessed by their skin-crawling powers.

DON'T DO THIS

Don't trust a yikari. Yikaria culture prizes deceit and betrayal. The kindest yikaria you meet will only be waiting for a chance to double-cross you.

Don't accept any food or drink. Anything they offer you is almost certainly poisoned.

BUILDING YOUR OWN DUNGEON

Traveling to remote dungeons and unlocking their secrets is rewarding, but even more exciting is the thrill of creating your own fiendish fortress or sunken stronghold. From initial idea to layout, treasure and traps, every part is yours to produce and populate.

When you close your eyes, what kind of dungeon do you see? Does it have ornate halls and spiral staircases, or are there twisting caverns made of rough-hewn rock? Is it a moss-covered ruin in a dense jungle, or a glittering ice-tower carved from a glacier?

In a world where magic and monsters are real, there are no limits, only new destinations to explore.

DUNGEON CONCEPT

When you set out to create your own dungeon, think about its function and the distinct features you can use to engage adventurers as they explore it. A goblin village isn't the same as a cloud giant's stronghold or a white dragon's lair. Each one would look different, feel different, and carry their own unique threats.

LOCATION

Figuring out where your dungeon is located will instantly start to narrow your focus and generate other ideas. Look to the following list of dungeon locales for inspiration, or come up with your own. The options are endless!

Behind a waterfall

Beneath a graveyard

Floating in the sky

In a cliff face

In catacombs beneath a city

In the desert

Inside a volcano

Underwater

CREATOR

Knowing who built this dungeon will also help you understand the size and scope of the place you're creating. And remember, whomever constructed it doesn't still have to be dwelling there. Many dungeons are abandoned and reused over the centuries.

Use any of the following potential creator options, or come up with something of your own invention.

A forgotten civilization

A wizard

An evil cult

Dwarves

Elves

Goblins

Smugglers

No creator at all (natural formations)

PURPOSE

Dungeons are built to fulfill an objective. Knowing what that is will help you define important areas within. Also, keep in mind that dungeons can be repeatedly abandoned and then repurposed by different occupants. A shrine can fall into ruin and become a lair, or a castle may have been struck by a dark plague and become a tomb.

Death Trap: A way to guard treasure or a competition to test the skills of warriors and wizards alike, a death trap is built to destroy any who enter.

Lair: A monster's living quarters and also a place where it can hoard its valuables. Be careful, a creature confronted in its home tends to fight with even more intensity than usual.

Mine: An active mine where rare ore, gemstones, or metals are harvested, or an abandoned mine occupied by creatures who thrive in the dark.

Stronghold: A secure base of operations for villains or monsters. A fortress like this is built with defense in mind, so a successful delve may involve infiltration rather than charging at the front entrance.

Temple or Shrine: Whether still active or now abandoned, this place was intended for worship and ritual.

Tomb: A resting place for the departed, along with their secrets and treasures.

POPULATING YOUR DUNGEON

What's a dungeon without monsters to fight? Start by choosing a few of your favorite foes, then use the following guidelines to help decide on the rest.

ECOLOGY

Areas where people or creatures gather have their own ecosystems. Creatures who live there need to eat, drink, breathe, and sleep. A king needs a throne room, but also a bedroom. Worshippers need places to pray. Soldiers need barracks and storage areas for their equipment. Are there areas still under construction or that have been closed off due to collapse, mold, or other issues that have arisen? When you set out to design a dungeon, you should think about the internal logic of the spaces you're creating and what the occupants need in order to carry out their day-to-day tasks—food preparation will probably be close to food storage, a guardhouse should be near the prison cells it watches over, or a hatchery placed by the sleeping area of a protective mother.

INHABITANTS

A dungeon is sometimes dominated by a single monster or a large group of intelligent creatures, but they don't have to be the sole occupants. Fungi, vermin, scavengers, and various predators can all coexist in the same space with the main inhabitants.

- Do the creatures controlling this dungeon have pets? If so, where are those pets kept and how are they fed?

- Do the occupants of this place take prisoners? Are those captives potential allies to you if they're freed?

- If a dungeon is quite large, are there multiple factions within vying for control?

- The ways in which all the dungeon's inhabitants interact will give you any number of story ideas.

TRAPS

Intentional and dangerous, traps are created to fool the unwary and stop their progress through a dungeon. These devices may be built to hurt or to hold, but they're always constructed to cause trouble.

Like the dungeon itself, when creating traps you must first decide who built them and what purpose they serve. It's rare that a trap would be set up in a space where denizens need to travel often, so think carefully about why it's been placed there and what lies beyond that's worth protecting.

Second, decide if the trap will be mechanical or magical in nature. Mechanical traps include basic ambush material such as pits or falling blocks, but can ramp up in complexity to whirling blades, flying arrows, flooding rooms, or clockwork puzzles. Magical traps cast a spell when activated and the effects can be almost anything you imagine: A floor trap could teleport the person who sets it off to another part of the dungeon.

Third, determine how the trap is triggered, what the effect will be, and how a group of adventurers might detect it if they were careful enough: Opening a door improperly could prompt a blast of magical fire to erupt into the hallway. Intelligent creatures who place traps in their lairs need ways to get past them without harming themselves. A trap might have a secret switch that disables its effect or an alternate route that adventurers can take to bypass it entirely.

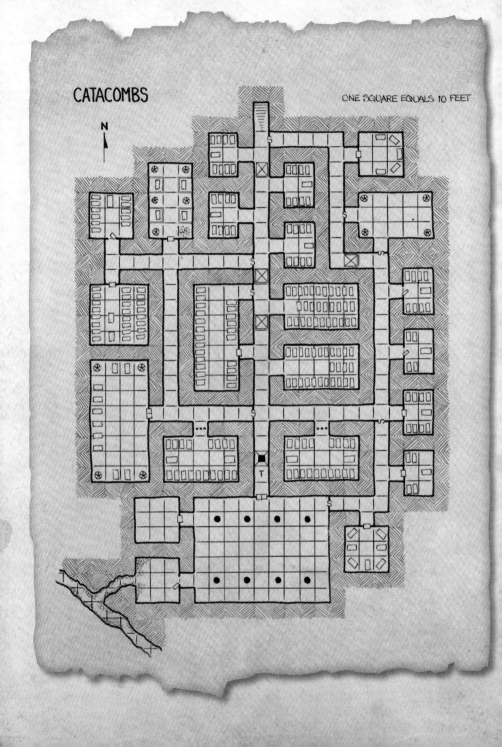

CATACOMBS

ONE SQUARE EQUALS 10 FEET

N

MAPMAKING

Having a concept, knowing the occupants, and creating a list of different areas are the perfect ingredients for building a dungeon. Now you need to start making a map!

A dungeon is most easily mapped on graph paper, with each square representing a standard measurement, such as five or ten feet per square. Use your key areas as starting points, then connect them with other features. As you plan, keep these points in mind.

- Symmetry is boring. If a group of adventurers explores one half of a dungeon, they'll rush through the second half if the layout is the same. Don't make your maps too predictable.

- Even if a dungeon is manually constructed, there are ways to incorporate indigenous features as well. Waterfalls, chasms, falling rocks, and other natural elements can provide interesting obstacles for your players.

- Using the grid is a nice way to get straight hallways and rectangular rooms, but don't be afraid to switch things up by varying the shape, size, and direction of your dungeon areas.

- Think about furniture and storage. How are the denizens using this space and what is needed to carry out daily tasks?

- Even though your map is two-dimensional, think in three dimensions. Use stairs, ramps, platforms, ledges, and balconies to add height or depth. It will make your dungeon more interesting than just having an endless series of level rooms.

- The ultimate goal within your dungeon will usually be as far from the entrance as possible, forcing adventurers deeper into danger and heightening the drama.

MAP SYMBOLS

Here are a series of standardized symbols you can use on your graph-paper maps to denote specific dungeon features. Mix and match them to bring to life the hidden places you've always imagined.

DOOR	TRAPDOOR IN CEILING
DOUBLE DOOR	TRAPDOOR IN FLOOR
SECRET DOOR	SECRET TRAPDOOR
ONE-WAY DOOR	OPEN PIT
ONE-WAY SECRET DOOR	COVERED PIT
FALSE DOOR	TRAP
REVOLVING DOOR	STAIRS
CONCEALED DOOR	STAIRS/SLIDE TRAP
ARCHWAY	SPIRAL STAIRS
OPEN DOORWAY	NATURAL STAIRS
PORTCULLIS OR BARS	LADDER

SLIDE		ROCK WALL
STATUE		PILLAR
WELL		ROCK COLUMN
POOL		STALACTITE
FOUNTAIN		STALAGMITE
DAIS		RUBBLE
ALTAR		CREVASSE
FIREPLACE		SINKHOLE
TABLE, CHEST		SUBMERGED PATH
BED		SUBTERRANEAN PASSAGE
CURTAIN		DEPRESSION
WINDOW		POND OR LAKE
ARROW SLIT		STREAM
RAILING		ELEVATED LEDGE
ILLUSIONARY WALL		NATURAL CHIMNEY

MAP EXAMPLES

The shrine of an evil cult where worshipers gather to make sacrifices, or a holy place of worship overrun by invading hordes that need to be cleared out by brave adventurers? You decide which one your adventuring party will face!

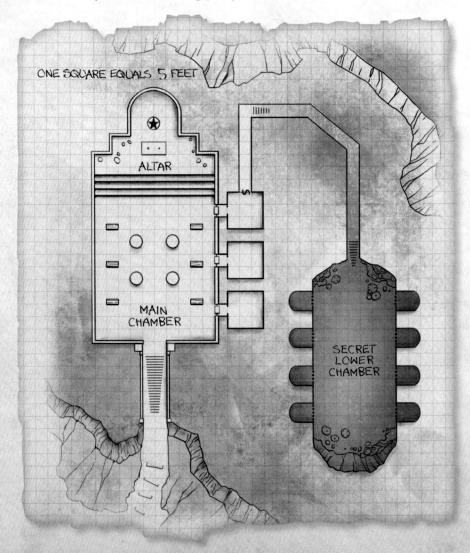

ONE SQUARE EQUALS 5 FEET

ALTAR

MAIN CHAMBER

SECRET LOWER CHAMBER

A haunted ship sailing through ghostly waters, or a pirate boat manned by cut-throat villains who have been terrorizing innocent farmers along the shoreline? Every map contains multiple possibilities, depending on how you decide to customize it!

EXPLORATION & QUESTS

How a dungeon experience begins and how it ends can contribute a great deal to making the journey through the space a memorable one. Epic fantasy stories don't start with someone merely opening a door and walking down a hallway. Use the entrance of your dungeon as a way to set expectations and to build excitement about the dangers and delights that lay ahead.

- What kind of journey is required to get to the dungeon? Is it close by or in a remote and inhospitable location?

- Is the entrance hidden? If so, what clues or methods must the adventurers use to find it?

- Is the entrance guarded? Who watches over this space and what will it take to get past them?

- Is the entrance locked? Is there a key, a magical phrase, or a trick used to gain access?

- Is the entrance magical? A teleportation circle may transport adventurers directly into the heart of a dungeon, or a permanent illusion may hide the safest entrance to a creature's lair.

- Is there more than one entrance? A fortress has a main gate, but there may be other smaller entry points for servants, shipping, or garbage disposal that adventurers can use to make their way inside. A cave may have a large opening at the base of a mountain, but there may be smaller tunnels at higher points as well.

Once a group has plumbed the depths of your dungeon, you'll want to make sure the final encounter is worthy of their time and effort. What kind of big set piece can you use and what foes can they face that will engage and excite them? What final obstacle must they overcome for their quest to be declared a success?

Are there any other tasks you can add to the final encounter beyond merely fighting a villain? Freeing prisoners, stopping a ritual, activating an ancient artifact, or undoing a curse can split the adventuring party's attention in a way that feels frantic and exciting. Maybe the final battle ends with the entire room crumbling as the floor gives way, sending the heroes plummeting toward an underground river that threatens to wash them away. Whatever you decide, make it exciting; because if you do, you and your friends can build stories together that you'll always remember.

TREASURE

At the end of every quest there must be a reward, a reason for adventurers to go through trials and tribulations while risking their health and happiness. For a cleric, that reward may be a renewal of faith after serving the needs of their deity. For a paladin, it may come in the form of pride from vanquishing evil. Along with satisfaction, conviction, and an overall sense of a job well done, the most common and appreciated form of compensation in a world of sword and sorcery is treasure. When you build your dungeon and populate it with dangers aplenty, you'll also want to decide what kind of wealth is available for plundering. Here are some ideas to get you started.

Art Objects: Idols or other sculptures, paintings, rare musical instruments, and even finely crafted dinnerware may be found and have value.

Coins: Simple and to the point. Gold, silver, and copper coins are the most common, but there are also rarer electrum and platinum ones to be considered as well.

Gemstones: Diamonds, rubies, sapphires, emeralds, amethysts, and dozens of other gems, plus brand-new crystal fascinations you come up with from your own imagination.

Jewelry: Necklaces, earrings, rings, bracelets, and other trinkets. Some may be kept and worn by adventurers while others can be traded or sold.

Knowledge: Rare books or scrolls, spell books, or alchemic recipes. For researchers and spellcasters, there may be information worth more than mere gold can purchase.

Magic Items: Wondrous items and enchanted objects are the kind of treasure many adventurers crave. Create your own or look to the *Wizards & Spells* guide for specific items to use.

New Adventure: A map to another destination, a mysterious code to be solved, or a journal detailing a villainous plot—sometimes the most valuable thing an explorer can find is a reason to keep exploring.

HOW MUCH IS TOO MUCH?

Receiving riches is a thrill, but be careful not to overload your dungeon with too much treasure. Magical items are less enchanting if a hero has a backpack full of them, and the desire to take on new expeditions can fade quickly if characters have more money than they know what to do with.

Keep in mind that the life of an adventurer does come with financial obligations. Armor needs to be repaired, clothes replaced, and weapons sharpened, and there are always local peasants in need who could use some of that newly unearthed gold to better their own lots in life. As a hero's legend begins to grow, their needs and expenses will rise to match their reputation.

USING DUNGEONS
TO TELL YOUR OWN STORIES

"The door is made of thick oak and reinforced with bands of metal."

"Is there a keyhole?"

"There is."

"Okay, Khylie will pull out her thieves' tools and spring that lock."

"Hold on a sec. I'm gonna shoulder-check the door and bust it open. We don't have time to sit around while she messes with finicky locks."

"Are you sure?"

"Yeah, absolutely. Dorbo tucks his head down, gets a running start, and charges at the door."

"I never actually said the door was locked . . . so you smash into the door and it instantly flies open. You're running full speed and weren't expecting it to give way so easily, so now you can't stop."

"Uh oh."

"You stumble a few feet, trip, and fall to the floor right in the middle of nine skeletons armed with rusty swords who were waiting for you on the other side. Their bones click and grind as they move in to attack."

Now that you've put together your own dungeon concept and sketched out a map, you're well on your way to becoming a Dungeon Master! What matters most is using your imagination and collaborating with your friends to create something new that you wouldn't have been able to come up with on your own.

Your idea might start with a one dungeon, but it can go *anywhere*: a creature's lair, the village nearby, cities and castles, caverns or skyscapes. You get to choose all the ingredients and stir them together. To help you as you develop your story, here are some questions to keep in mind:

WHO ARE YOUR CHARACTERS?

- Are your heroes like you or different? Young or old, human or something else? Think about the foes you must face. Great heroes require great challenges. What makes your villains memorable and powerful, and what brings them into conflict with your adventurers?

WHERE DOES YOUR STORY TAKE PLACE?

- At the top of a mountain, in a serene forest, deep underwater, or in a creepy boneyard?

WHEN DOES THE STORY HAPPEN?

- At night or during the day, in the middle of a thunderstorm or right before the bells toll to ring in the new year? Think about time passing as your story unfolds.

HOW DO THINGS CHANGE AS THE STORY PROCEEDS?

- Do your heroes succeed or fail? Do they find somewhere new or explore someplace old?

WHAT SHOULD SOMEONE FEEL AS THEY EXPERIENCE YOUR STORY?

- Do you want them to laugh or get scared? Cheer or be grossed out?

WHY ARE YOUR HEROES GOING ON THIS ADVENTURE?

- Knowing what their goals are will help you create a compelling tale of heroism and exploration.

Remember, you don't have to answer all these questions by yourself! Dungeons & Dragons is a collaborative game where you work with your friends to create your own stories. One person acts as a narrator, called a Dungeon Master, and the other players each take on the role of a hero, called a Player Character, in the adventuring party in a story. The Dungeon Master sets up a scene by describing a place and any threats that may exist, and then each player contributes ideas by explaining their own character's actions. With each scene created by the group, the story moves forward in unexpected and entertaining ways.

If you don't feel confident starting from scratch, you can go to your local gaming store and play a Dungeons & Dragons demonstration session. Demos can be a quick way to learn how the game is played and an opportunity to possibly make some brand-new friends at the same time.

After you've read through all the environs in this little dungeon document, there's even more Dungeons & Dragons material to ignite your imagination. The *Monsters & Creatures* guide is bursting at the seams with beasts aplenty for you and your friends to defeat. *Warriors & Weapons* goes into more detail about the different adventuring races and the martial classes who can join you on your quest. And the *Wizards & Spells* guide is filled with mystical magic to aid in your exploits. You know what dangerous places are to be found out there in the darkness, now figure out who your hero will be and *go forth on an adventure!*

Published in the United States by Ten Speed Press, an imprint of Random House, a division of Penguin Random House LLC, New York.
www.tenspeed.com

Ten Speed Press and the Ten Speed Press colophon are registered trademarks of Penguin Random House LLC.

Library of Congress Cataloging-in-Publication Data is on file with the publisher.

Hardcover ISBN: 978-1-9848-5644-9
eBook ISBN: 978-1-9848-5645-6

Printed in China

Publisher: Aaron Wehner
Art Director and Designer: Betsy Stromberg
Editor: Julie Bennett
Managing Editor: Doug Ogan
Production Designer: Lisa Bieser
Wizards of the Coast Team: David Gershman, Kate Irwin, Adam Lee, Hilary Ross, Liz Schuh
Illustrations: Conceptopolis, LLC
Ravenloft Cards (page 34): Chuck Lukacs

10 9 8 7 6 5 4 3 2 1

First Edition